THIS BOOK
BELONGS TO:

Get Ready to Fall in Love with Snowflakes!

Unleash your creativity and bring the magic of winter to life! This enchanting coloring book is filled with intricate and delicate snowflakes, each one unique and waiting to be transformed by your colorful touch.

Not only will you have fun coloring these beautiful designs, but you can also cut them out and use them as decorations for your windows, walls, or gifts. Imagine the joy of creating your own snowflake wonders to brighten up your winter days!

So grab your favorite colors and let it snow...

Wave Motion

THANK YOU FOR BRINGING A TOUCH OF WINTER MAGIC INTO YOUR LIFE WITH OUR SNOWFLAKES COLORING BOOK!

WE HOPE YOU HAD AS MUCH FUN COLORING AND CREATING WITH THESE DELICATE DESIGNS AS WE DID BRINGING THEM TO YOU. IF YOU ENJOYED THIS BOOK, PLEASE CONSIDER LEAVING A GOOD REVIEW ON AMAZON TO HELP OTHERS DISCOVER THE JOY OF SNOWFLAKE COLORING.

YOUR FEEDBACK MEANS THE WORLD TO US!

Wave Motion

Made in the USA
Monee, IL
17 December 2024

74162479R00057